Gurney's Gallery
of Dogs

Gurney's Gallery of Dogs

And
Doggie Dictionary

By
Eric Gurney

*One Hundred Twelve Plus One
Breeds of Dogs are Shown Inside . . .*

Published by
Woodbridge Press / *Santa Barbara, California*

Published and distributed by

Woodbridge Press Publishing Company
Post Office Box 6189
Santa Barbara, California 93160

Copyright © 1983 by Eric Gurney

Distributed simultaneously in the United States and Canada

Printed in the United States of America

Library of Congress Cataloging in Publication Data

Gurney, Eric.
  Gurney's Gallery of dogs and doggie dictionary.

  Includes index.
    1. Dogs—Caricatures and cartoons. 2. Dog breeds. 3. American wit and humor, Pictorial. I. Title. II. Title: Gallery of dogs and doggie dictionary.
SF430.G87   1983   636.7   83-17081
ISBN 0-88007-137-0
ISBN 0-88007-138-9 (pbk.)

Dedicated to Hayden Barile,
Ethan, Skye, and Kyle Gurney,
and Colin and Lara Engler

Contents

Introduction

One whiff of barbequed buffalo meat and a dog tippy-toed to the entrance of a cave where a man was busy cooking. It didn't take this part-wolf and part-jackal long to beg for a handout and it didn't take the neolithic cave man long to oblige by tossing a juicy bone to this begging creature. It was a spectacular catch! It turned out to be the start of a beautiful friendship. Soon the dog and man were hunting together and both were eating high off the hog or mastodon—whatever the chef's choice of the day happened to be.

It was a **spectacular** catch!

In due time the dog acquired a mate who was also welcomed by the members of the cave family and, faster than you can say *canis familiaris*, she presented them with some roly poly puppies.

Man discovered that some dogs had very special talents that could be used for his benefit; to name a few—the strong dogs, those fleet of foot, the keen of smell, the sharp of eyesight, the diggers, and the great chewers. A good use for the latter is still to be worked out.

At that time—when you lived a stone's throw from your nearest neighbor and you usually carried the bump on your head to prove it—a strong, brave watchdog was much appreciated, to guard the family and supplies.

Because much of the dog's family tree is about as clear as

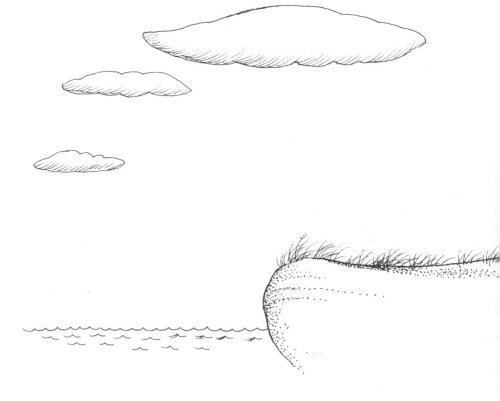

the Newfoundland fog banks on a moonless night, one can only touch on the highlights of a few thousand years.

During this period of time man coaxed, cajoled, and made friends with many specialists in dogdom. For instance, dogs that, though slow of movement, had extra-keen scenting powers were selected and bred to track down the larger game; while those of great strength and keen hearing were used for guard duty.

An unwary trespasser, believing that "barking dogs never bite," soon became painfully aware of the true facts. He also may have been the first person to run the hundred yards in ten seconds flat—and all this with the added handicap of a good-sized dog latched on to his rear end.

From just three or four special divisions of dogs descended the hundreds of distinct breeds we know today.

*He also may have been the first person
to run the hundred yards in ten seconds flat!*

The Shaggiest Dogs

1. Affenpinscher

2. Old English
    Sheepdog

3. Briard

4. Otter Hound

5. Puli

13

Dogs with Tails that Curl Over Their Backs

8. Norwegian Elkhound

6. Shih Tzu

7. Lhasa Apso

9. Samoyed

10. Keeshond

11. Chow Chow

12. Basenji

13. Pug

Sheep Dogs

14. Border Collie

15. Komondor

19. Belgian Sheepdog

22. Rottweiler

18. Shetland Sheepdog

21. Belgian Tervuren

16. Bearded Collie

17. Collie

20. Belgian Malinois

The Smallest Dogs

23. Chihuahua

24. Maltese

25. Pomeranian

26. Yorkshire Terrier

27. American Water Spaniel

28. Curly-coated Retriever

29. Bedlington Terrier

Dogs with Curly Coats

(Long-haired Dachshund with curlers)

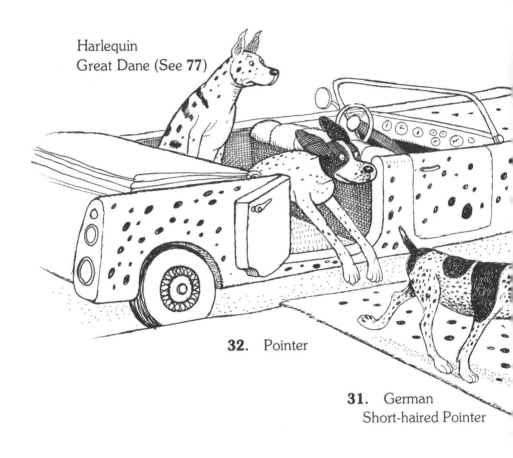

Harlequin
Great Dane (See **77**)

32. Pointer

31. German
Short-haired Pointer

Dogs with Spots

30. Dalmatian

Dogs with the Most Handsome Beards

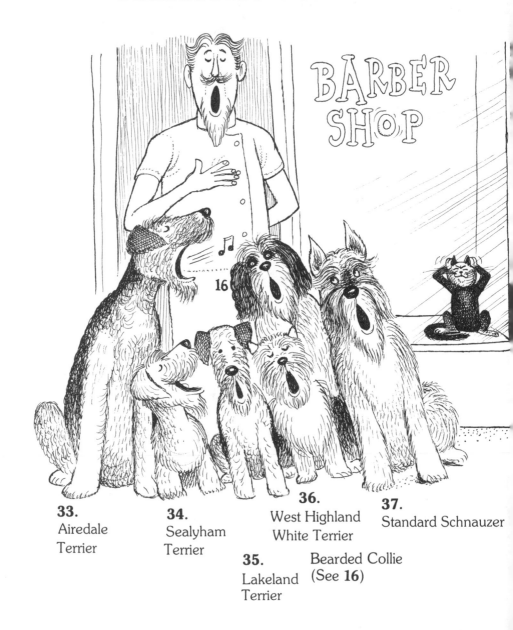

33.
Airedale
Terrier

34.
Sealyham
Terrier

35.
Lakeland
Terrier

36.
West Highland
White Terrier

37.
Standard Schnauzer

Bearded Collie
(See **16**)

38. Wire-haired Fox Terrier

39.
Kerry Blue Terrier

40. Welsh Terrier

41.
Bouvier
des Flandres

42. Scottish Terrier

...more Terriers

43. Border Terrier

44. Cairn Terrier

45. Silky Terrier

46. Australian Terrier

47. Irish Terrier

48. Norwich Terrier

49. Manchester Terrier

50. Smooth Fox Terrier

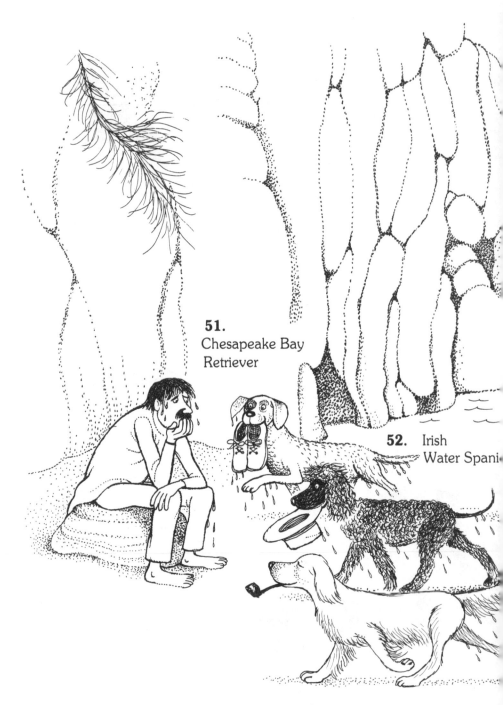

51.
Chesapeake Bay
Retriever

52. Irish
Water Spani

53. Golden Retriever

The Retrievers

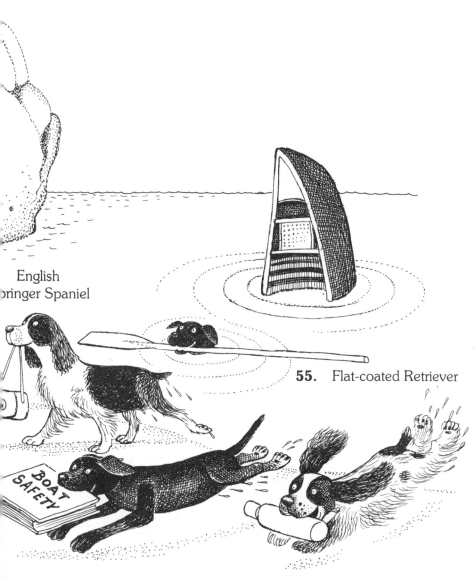

English
Springer Spaniel

55. Flat-coated Retriever

BOAT SAFETY

56. Labrador Retriever

57. Cocker Spaniel

58. Whippet

59. Greyhound

The Fastest Dogs

60. Afghan Hound

61. Saluki

The Greatest Sniffers

62. Foxhound

63. Basset Hound

64. Black and Tan Coonhound

Smooth Dachshund (See **68**)

65. Beagle

66. Bloodhound

Dogs with the Shortest Legs

67. Long-haired Dachshund

68. Smooth Dachshund

69. Wire-haired Dachshund

71. Welsh Corgi
(Cardigan, Pembroke)

70. Dandie Dinmont Terrier

Dogs with Flat Faces

72. Bulldog

73. Pekingese

Pug (See **13**)

74. Boston Terrier

75. French Bulldog

76. Japanese Spaniel

The Tallest Dogs

77. Great Dane

78. Scottish Deerhound

79. Borzoi (Russian Wolfhound)

80. Irish Wolfhound

81. Kuvasz

Guard Dogs

82. Bull Mastiff

83. Mastiff

84. Doberman Pinscher

85. German Shepherd

86. Giant Schnauzer

The Pointers

87. English Setter

88. Gordon Setter

32. Pointer

89. Brittany Spaniel

90. Vizsla

91. Irish Setter

92. Weimaraner

93. Wire-haired Pointing Griffon

43

94. Great Pyrenees

95. Newfoundland

83. Mastiff

44

The Heaviest Dogs

YOUR
WEIGHT

96. St. Bernard Long-haired

(Also: Mastiff, 83; Otter Hound, 4; Great Dane, 77; and Irish Wolfhound, 80)

112. American Staffordshire Terrier

97. Schipperke

98. Siberian Husky

111. Bernese Mountain Dog

110. Sussex Spaniel
(Losing a few points)

109. Rhodesian Ridgeback

108. Harrier

107. Alaskan Malamute

99. Welsh Springer Spaniel

100. Bull Terrier

The Dog Show

101. Poodle

102. English Toy Spaniel

103. Italian Greyhound

106. Short-haired St. Bernard

104. Brussels Griffon

105. Papillon

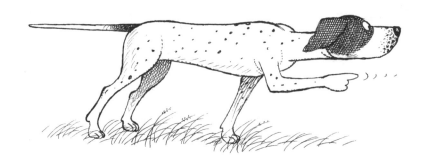

Doggie Dictionary

This dictionary has "one hundred and twelve plus one" different breeds of dogs. The American Kennel Club recognizes 115 breeds and the English Kennel Club, 105. (It is pretty tough for a person like me who can't spell to look a word up in the dictionary. I have to turn into a Sherlock Holmes to finally track it down.)

In this "dictionary" the dog categories are the same as those in the first part of this book—the "Gallery"—and every dog has the same number it has there. In this Doggie Dictionary every dog has its description, alongside, or underneath, its picture.

These dogs are, for the most part, as thoroughbred as the British Royal Family. Others are such top dogs that they had to be included. For instance, the Border Collie is shown in the nation's top shows for its ability in rounding up sheep.

There is a reason for even the strangest breeds of dogs. Some were developed for their great sniffing ability; others as wonderful watch dogs. There are dogs to point out game and others to retrieve. These reasons are just part of what you will discover in this Doggie Dictionary.

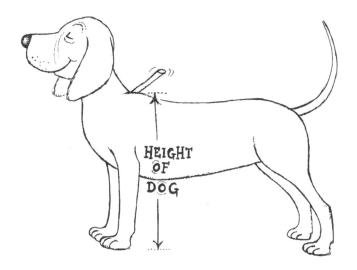

HEIGHT
OF
DOG

How To Measure Your Dog

The height of a dog is reckoned as shoulder height. Don't
trust trying to measure old Rover by using your two hands like
you were showing off the size of the fish you caught. By the
time you walk over to the measuring stick your hands will have
spread apart five or six more inches. Place your dog broadside
against the wall. Where its neck joins the body, balance the
stick and mark the spot where the stick touches the wall. From
there to the floor will give you the height.

How To Weigh Your Dog

The big trick in weighing your dog is to be able to get a clear view of the weight indicator while old Bozo is kicking and struggling to get out of your arms. After you find your combined weights, you weigh yourself and subtract your weight from the combined weights and the difference is the dog's weight.

The Shaggiest Dogs

1

Affenpinscher

Weighs 8 pounds and is 10 inches high at the shoulder.

This little dog looks like a miniature Gay Nineties bouncer with moustache and goatee included. He is absolutely fearless and will take on anything from King Kong to the Jolly Green Giant. He has a very short, dense, shaggy coat.

2

Old English Sheep Dog

Weighs 50 to 65 pounds; height, 21 to 25 inches.

You wonder how this dog could see through the hair over its eyes well enough to drive sheep and cattle to marketplaces in the cities. Well, it could. It was an expert and was called a drover's dog. The beautiful thing about this gorgeous animal was that it was exempt from taxes.

3
Briard

Weighs 70 to 80 pounds; height, 22 to 27 inches.

In France, the Briard is top dog in guarding small farms.
Herding sheep and cattle, and generally keeping an eye on
everything that needs protecting. They also have a great record
as war dogs. They were able to take advantage of their acute
hearing in sneaking past enemy lines with supplies.

4
Otter Hound

Weighs 75 to 115 pounds; height, 24 to 27 inches.

With its oily coat and webbed feet, the Otter Hound was the
king of the ponds in the 1800's in England, where he was used
to kill otters. At that time the otters were eating up all the choice
fish before the fishermen could even cast their hooks into the
water.

5

Puli

Weighs about 35 pounds and is about 17 inches high.

This dog has been Mr. Big in the lives of Hungarian shepherds for more than one thousand years. (For some weird reason sheep take direction more easily from dark-colored dogs.) The Puli's habit of running over the sheep's backs to take a shortcut is certainly the sign of a thinking dog.

Dogs with Tails that Curl Over Their Backs

6

Shi Tzu

Weighs 9 to 18 pounds and is about 10 inches high.

This little dog has become known to us through the paintings made of it during the T'ang Dynasty in China. Shi Tzu means lion. A full-size lion could swallow a Shi Tzu like a tasty fortune cookie.

7

Lhasa Apso

Weighs 15 lbs and is 10 inches high.

In the mysterious land of Tibet near mighty Mount Everest lives this great little dog known as the "Bark Lion Sentinel Dog," which is a very long-winded title for such a little critter. Because of its intelligence and acute hearing it is kept as a special guard inside dwellings. It is very easily trained and responsive to love and kindness.

8

Norwegian Elkhound

Weighs about 50 pounds and is 18 to 20 inches high.

This loyal dog has been a real pal to man for thousands of years. Along with the early Vikings it hunted bear and wolves. With a little imagination we can see its ears turning into steer horns and forming an ancient Viking helmet.

9

Samoyed

Weighs about 36 pounds and is 23 inches high.

The Samoyed (pronounced Sam-a-yed) is another great companion of man and helped make possible the discovery of the North and South Poles. It has a unique, good-natured disposition and has the happy expression of one who has just won a lottery.

10
Keeshound

Weighs about 35 pounds and is 17 to 18 inches high.

This dog is from Holland and was known as the Barge Dog. It even has the stance of a ship's captain standing on the bridge of his beautiful boat. It is a great companion and couldn't care less for hunting. He probably wouldn't move a muscle if a rabbit jumped over his back.

11
Chow Chow

Weighs 50 to 60 pounds and is 19 to 20 inches high.

The Chow Chow has a tongue that looks as if he eats nothing but huckleberries all day long. He is very aloof and has an air of being ticked off all the time. Years ago in China it was used as a hunting dog because of its great scenting powers and clever hunting tactics.

12

Basenji

Weighs 22 to 24 pounds and is 16 to 17 inches high.

Baying to a full moon means nothing to this wonderful dog, because it is known as the barkless dog. It is one of the oldest breeds and was given as presents to the Pharoahs of ancient Egypt. It was a great hunter, due to its speed, power, and silence.

13

Pug

Weighs 14 to 18 pounds and is 10 to 11 inches high.

The Pug looks a lot like the manager of a prizefighter despite the fact that it came originally from behind the Great Wall of China where wrestling was the big sport. It is sometimes called the "Dutch Pug," which leads one to think, mistakenly, that it was indigenous to Holland.

Sheep Dogs

14

Border Collie

Weighs 45 pounds and is 18 inches high.

The Border Collie can round up sheep faster than a hungry anteater can lap up a colony of ants. When it comes to competing in obedience trials it usually trots home decked in blue ribbons plus a beautiful silver cup.

15

Komondor

Weighs up to 90 pounds and is 23 to 27 inches high.

Although this dog looks like a king-size mop in his natural habitat, he is an absolutely handsome dog when reared in kennels and groomed for dog shows. In his native Hungary he is used as a protector rather than a herder.

16
Bearded Collie

It is 28 inches high and weighs about 60 pounds.

This dog's coat is like an extra-large doormat, although a beautiful one. Put a pipe in its mouth and a tweed hat on its head and it would look like a distinguished old gentleman.

17
Collie

Weighs 50 to 60 pounds and is 22 to 26 inches high.

More has been written about this dog than any other breed and many movies have been produced with the Collie in the leading role. It can take hand signals like a professional and, if need be, could probably smile and form the word "cheese" as well as the most glamorous actress in Hollywood.

18

Shetland Sheepdog

Weighs 16 pounds and is 13 to 16 inches high.

If you could look at a rough Collie through a reducing glass you would see before you a Shetland Sheepdog, with very slight differences other than size. These delightful dogs from the Shetland Islands of Scotland are charming, alert, docile, very agile and above all, exceptionally intelligent.

19

Belgian Sheepdog

Weighs 55 to 60 pounds and is 23 inches high.

To begin with, these dogs had coats of many colors and, without the selective breeding of a Professor Reul, they may have become the first plaid dog in history. However, they became long-haired and black; a perfect color for the police work they were put to when they first came to America in 1907.

20

Belgian Malinois

Weighs 55 to 60 pounds and is 23 inches high.

If the Malinois and the Belgian Sheepdog were standing in front of each other you would think the Malinois was looking in the mirror. The only difference is, the Sheepdog is black and the Malinois is fawn or mahogany and has a dense, short coat.

21

Belgian Tervuren

Weighs 55 to 60 pounds and is 23 inches high

This dog is also the spitting image of the Belgian Sheepdog except for its deep, rich, fawn coloring. The tip of each hair is black and it has a long and abundant coat.

22

Rottweiler

Weighs 80 to 90 pounds and is 22 to 27 inches high.

About two thousand years ago these large, impressive dogs had to take orders in Italian, but later on, when the Romans conquered the German township of Rottweil and left the dogs there, they had to switch to understanding and barking in German. Besides herding sheep, the Rottweiler was great as a guard dog. It was the custom for the master to tie his purse around the dog's neck, as few bandits cared to tangle with this powerful dog and come out second best.

The Smallest Dogs

23
Chihuahua

Weighs 1 to 6 pounds and is about 5 inches high.

This little dog is Numero Uno when it comes to being the smallest of all dogs. It was named after the Mexican state of Chihuahua. The dogs were first found living in some old ruins close to the Casas Grandes River.

24
Maltese

Weighs 2 to 7 pounds and is about 5 inches high.

For more than three thousand years this tiny dog has been living high off the hog. It was named for the Island of Malta in the Mediterranean Sea. If it had all its hair clipped off it would be about as big as a squirrel.

25

Pomeranian

Weighs 3 to 7 pounds and is 7 inches high.

This lively little dog came into being in Pomerania, in old
Prussia, where it was bred down in size from the large white
Spitz. You would wonder how such a small animal as the
Pomeranian could have such a bountiful crop of hair. I am sure
a lot of bald men would love to know the secret.

26

Yorkshire Terrier

Weighs 4 to 8 pounds and is 8 to 9 inches high.

This terrier and the famous pudding were both named for the
English county of Yorkshire. If it is a show dog, its coat will be
as well protected as the Hope diamond. Even its feet must be
booted to keep them from scratching and ruining its glorious
coat.

Dogs with the Curliest Coats

27

American Water Spaniel

Weighs 25 to 45 pounds and is 15 to 18 inches high.

As a retriever, this dog is top-notch. In the swimming department it would give Tarzan a swim for his money. If women had curls like this Water Spaniel they would never need to spend money at the hairdresser's for a permanent.

28

Curly-coated Retriever

Weighs 70 to 80 pounds and is 15 to 18 inches high.

This great water dog has curls on top of curls, which help to shed water. One quick shake of that curly coat and in seconds it is as dry as a stone on the Sahara Desert.

29
Bedlington Terrier
Weighs 22 to 24 pounds and is 15 to 17 inches high.

Named for the shire of Bedlington in England, where it was famous for hunting rats, this terrier could snap a rat's neck faster than a bullet fired from a Colt 45.

Dogs with Spots

30

Dalmatian

Weighs 35 to 50 pounds and is 19 to 23 inches high.

This Austrian dog from the former province of Dalmatia loves horses like an Englishman loves roast beef. It has the appearance of a white dog that took a nap under a writer's desk while he was flicking black ink to make his pen flow better. The English nicknamed this dog the "coach" and the "firehouse dog."

31

German Short-haired Pointer

Weighs about 45 pounds and is 21 to 25 inches high.

Here is a jack-of-all-trades and master-of-all. This dog is intelligent, has a keen nose, is a great duck hunter, a natural retriever, a great watchdog and an excellent companion. And with its water-repellent coat and webbed feet could do well with the Aquacades.

32
Pointer

Weighs 55 to 60 pounds and is 24 to 25 inches high.

The Pointer has been used as a hunting dog in jolly old England since 1650. It will turn into a living statue in the middle of a stride and will stay that way, pointing at a bird, while spiders weave their webs around it. One man timed his dog in a pointing position for well over an hour.

Dogs with the Most Handsome Beards

33

Airedale Terrier

Weighs 17 to 35 pounds and is about 23 inches high.

If you cast your eagle eye on a few antique paintings from the land that made Beefeater gin famous—namely, England—you will see dogs that look mighty like Airedales. Airedales are used to hunt game in Africa, India, Canada, and the United States.

34

Sealyham Terrier

Weighs 21 pounds and is 10 inches high.

This Terrier derives its name from Sealyham, Haverford West in Wales. Its digging ability would come in mighty handy for a diamond miner. Instead, this skill is used for going underground and doing battle with all sorts of critters like fox, rabbits, badgers and otters.

35

Lakeland Terrier

Weighs 15 to 17 pounds and is 14 inches high.

It seems as if every Fido, Rover, and Spot were originally trained to guard against the raids of the fox and otter, and the Lakeland Terrier is no exception. This dog has the courage of a lion tamer who has lost his whip and has been known to follow an otter for 20 feet underground. It was born, raised, and worked in the Lake District of England.

36

West Highland White Terrier

Weighs 13 to 19 pounds and is 10 to 11 inches high.

This jaunty little dog might become quite conceited if it knew that it and a cousin, the Scottish Terrier, were on the labels of millions of whiskey bottles advertising Black and White Scotch. They are very hardy dogs and love to play in the snow and will follow skaters for miles across frozen lakes.

37
Standard Schnauzer

Weighs 35 pounds and is 17 to 20 inches high.

This is a German breed of great antiquity and, in certain poses, looks like the famous writer, George Bernard Shaw. Its portrait has been painted by Albrecht Dürer, Rembrandt and Sir Joshua Reynolds. The principal duty of this dog was to be a rat catcher and a guard. Schnauzer comes from schnauze, meaning muzzle, and schnauzbart, meaning moustache.

38

Wire-haired Fox Terrier

Weighs 15 to 19 pounds and is 15 inches high.

This is an English breed of ancient origin and looks exactly like a Smooth Fox Terrier that has taken shots of tonic to grow hair. This is one lively little dog that derives its name from the days when it was brought in to dig the fox out of its hiding place.

39
Kerry Blue Terrier
Weighs 30 to 40 pounds and is 17 to 20 inches high.

You would think that because it comes from Ireland, this dog should be green rather than blue—especially since it is the national dog of that country. It was first noticed in the mountainous regions of County Kerry and was given the name Kerry Blue.

40
Welsh Terrier
Weighs about 20 pounds and stands 15 inches high.

It looks like an Airedale Terrier that spent too much time in a steam bath and lost about 25 pounds. These dogs originated in Wales and were then, as now, sporting dogs. They make fine pets.

41

Bouvier des Flandres

Weighs about 70 pounds and is 23 to 27 inches high.

If you ever see a member of the Belgian police force lifting its leg on a fire hydrant you will know that it is none other than a Bouvier des Flandres. A Bouvier cannot win the title of "Champion" unless it has also won prizes in work competitions, such as duty in police, army, and defense units.

42

Scottish Terrier

Weighs 18 to 22 pounds and is about 10 inches high.

When you hear someone calling, "Here, Mactavish," you will know know that a Scottish Terrier is coming around the corner. In fact, you can almost hear the bagpipes blowing as he walks with his kilt-like coat swishing from side to side.

...more Terriers

43

Border Terrier

Weighs 11½ to 15½ pounds and is 12 to 13 inches high.

Foxes had to be extra smart to outwit the vast number of dogs trained to hunt them. One of their oldest enemies is the Border Terrier from the Scottish border. It can climb a wall like a fly and scramble through wire entanglements like a spy. But for all that it is particularly gentle with children.

44

Cairn Terrier

Weighs 13 to 15 pounds and is 9 to 10 inches high.

The Cairn Terrier came from the cairns or the rocky, wild shores of the Isle of Skye, Scotland, where its rock-hopping ability made it look as if it were attached to springs. There, these hardy little dogs proved their value by their determined efforts to destroy all vermin and an occasional fox, badger, or otter.

45
Silky Terrier

Weighs 8 to 10 pounds and is 9 to 10 inches high.

This dog's coat is so glamorous that any of the 10 best-dressed women in the world would be delighted to own one as nice. The Silky Terrier was developed in Sydney, Australia, as a companion for apartment dwellers.

46
Australian Terrier

Weighs 12 to 14 pounds and is about 10 inches high.

This agile little terrier can kill a rabbit or a rat as fast as an eye can blink. It can also send a snake to its happy hunting ground by leaping straight up into the air, seizing it by the neck, and giving it a good shake.

47

Irish Terrier

Weighs 25 to 27 pounds and is about 18 inches high.

This terrier struts around like it owns the whole of Ireland, its
native land. It really has reason to do a bit of strutting as it is
top dog when it comes to ratting, rabbitting, fox hunting, and
badger baiting. Besides all this, deep down inside, it is a
good-natured, warm-hearted dog.

48

Norwich Terrier

Weighs 10 to 15 pounds and is 9 to 10 inches high.

Students of Cambridge College in England were instrumental
in popularizing the Norwich Terrier, which was then called the
Jones Terrier. It became a fad to own one. You could put a
mortar board on its head and it would pass for one of the
professors of that era. There is a drop-eared variety called the
Norfolk Terrier.

49

Manchester Terrier

Weighs 12 to 22 pounds and is 16 inches high.

The Pied Piper would never be needed to get rid of rats if the Manchester Terriers of England were available. One famous dog, Billy, held the rat-killing record. In less than six minutes he destroyed 100 large rats in a wooden-sided pit. That comes to about 3½ seconds per rat.

50

Smooth Fox Terrier

Weighs 15 to 19 pounds and is 14½ to 15½ inches high.

This Fox Terrier also gets its name from digging foxes out of their lairs. It looks exactly like a Wire-haired Fox Terrier with its hair clipped.

The Retrievers

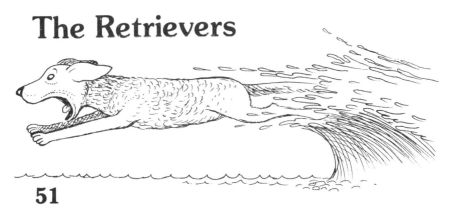

51

Chesapeake Bay Retriever

Weighs 55 to 75 pounds and is 21 to 26 inches high.

This is a super water dog with webbed feet like a duck and it can swim in icy water like a polar bear. The breed was started when a couple of Newfoundland puppies were rescued from a wrecked English brig off the coast of Maryland and mated to local retrievers.

52

Irish Water Spaniel

Weighs 45 to 65 pounds and is 21 to 24 inches high.

With its crazy-looking topknot you can well imagine this dog putting on a clown act with your favorite T.V. comedian. It is related to the Portuguese Water Dog and is a maniac when it comes to swimming and diving. It will retrieve anything, including an escaped fish, with the speed of a seal. It is a remarkable all-round retriever.

53

Golden Retriever

Weighs 55 to 75 pounds and is 20 to 24 inches high.

The first Golden Retrievers were bred from a Flat-coated Retriever and a liver-colored Spaniel. The puppies were so beautiful their British owner named them Crocus, Primrose, Cowslip, and Ada. Before the echo of the hunter's gun blast has faded the Golden Retriever is carefully bringing back the kill. They also make wonderful pets.

54

English Springer Spaniel

Weighs 42 to 50 pounds and is 17 to 19 inches high.

This is one of the best tail waggers in all Dogdom. If we could attach a fan to its tail we could save a lot of electricity. It is the daddy of the Spaniel clan and is both a highly successful show dog and an attractive family pet.

55

Flat-coated Retriever

Weighs 60 to 70 pounds and is 23 inches high.

Most hunting dogs were so specialized they would do their own particular job and then call it a day. There were dogs to point and dogs to spring the birds into the air but no dogs to retrieve. One of the first to be trained to fetch the quarry was the Flat-coated Retriever.

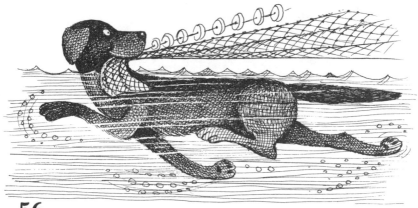

56

Labrador Retriever

Weighs 55 to 75 pounds and is 22 to 24 inches high.

When first heard of in 1822, this dog worked for the Newfoundland fishermen. It would dive overboard and drag the ends of the nets to the men on shore who would pull them in. It did everything but pick up a paycheck. But it was quite a while before it was trained to assist the hunter in picking up game from the water.

57

Cocker Spaniel

The English Cocker weighs 28 to 35 pounds and is 15 inches high.
The American Cocker weighs 22 to 28 pounds and is 14 inches high.

Part of this dog's name comes from Spain, where it may have originated, and the "Cocker" is from England, where it was used for woodcock hunting. This little dog could have written Dale Carnegie's "How To Win Friends and Influence People," because it is one of the world's friendliest dogs. It could have charmed Ebenezer Scrooge.

The Fastest Dogs

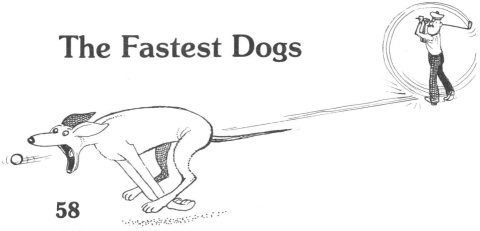

58

Whippet

Weighs 13 to 18 pounds and is 18 to 22 inches high.

This English-bred dog can run 100 yards in 6 seconds flat and would make a man feel like he was running backwards. Whippet racing began among miners in the coal fields at the turn of the century. It was called "poor man's horse racing."

59

Greyhound

Weighs 60 to 70 pounds and is 27 inches high.

This dog was around several thousand years before the Christian era. It was used by the Pharaohs of Egypt for hunting. There is a wealth of pictorial history on this dog because well-to-do owners commissioned artists and sculptors to immortalize Dear Old Fido on the walls of their tombs. The Greyhound of today is not only a racing star but an excellent pet as well.

60
Afghan Hound

Weighs 50 to 60 pounds and is 24 to 28 inches high.

Some authorities are adamant about the fact that it was an
Afghan that trotted up the gangplank with its mate into Noah's
ark. This aristocratic dog, with its watchspring of a tail, loved to
hunt gazelles just as much as it loved snoozing on its owner's
best silken cushions.

61
Saluki

Weighs 60 pounds and is 22 to 28 inches high.

This dog was just about as royal as a dog could be in ancient
Egypt and its likeness is painted in many of the Pharoahs'
tombs. It can run so fast it makes a gazelle look like its feet were
stuck in cement.

The Greatest Sniffers

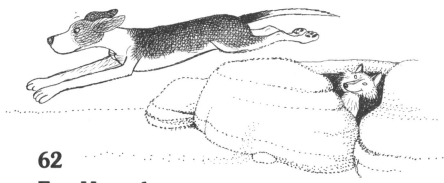

62
Fox Hound

Weighs 60 to 70 pounds and is 21 to 25 inches high.

When the Fox Hound takes up the trail of the fox it lets forth a mighty howl that would rival the lead tenor at the opera. Hunters are able to identify the voices of their own hounds as they pursue the wily fox.

63
Basset Hound

Weighs 25 to 45 pounds and is 11 to 15 inches high.

When you hear howling in close harmony with the hunter's horn you know it is the Basset Hound. It is probably still howling in French as France is where it originated. Despite its solemn-looking countenance, it is a clown. With the exception of the Bloodhound there is no breed with greater scenting ability.

64

Black and Tan Coonhound

Weighs 50 to 60 pounds and is 23 to 27 inches high.

If you hear a sniffing sound that sounds like an old-fashioned steam locomotive, chances are a Black and Tan Coonhound has just crossed your path. Specializing in trailing and treeing the raccoon, it also trails almost any other kind of four-footed game. The coon dog is a mongrel but the Coonhound is a purebred.

65

Beagle

Weighs 18 to 30 pounds and there are two sizes; the first is under 13 inches; the other, from 13 to 15 inches.

The Beagle is a descendant of the scent hounds that cavorted around in the days of England's King Arthur. Their soft musical voices would make the lead trumpet player of the New York Philharmonic envious.

66

Bloodhound

Weighs 80 to 110 pounds and is 23 to 27 inches high.

This soulful-looking dog has just about the keenest sense of smell of anything on four legs. It can get a whiff of that roast beef you are cooking from a block away. Tracking—not attacking—is its sole aim and once it has found its quarry it is more likely to lick it than bite it.

(Also: Dachshund, 67-69)

Dogs with the Shortest Legs

67
Long-haired Dachshund

Weighs 5 to 20 pounds and is 5 to 9 inches high.

In Germany it is pronounced Docks-Hoond, which means "badger dog." There are standard and miniature sizes in long-haired, smooth, and wire-haired. The Dachshund is the third most popular dog in the United States.

68
Smooth Dachshund

Weighs 5 to 20 pounds and is 5 to 9 inches high.

This droll little dog looks just like a Long-haired Dachshund that was sheared for the summer season.

69
Wire-haired Dachshund
Weighs 5 to 20 pounds and is 5 to 9 inches high.

This debonaire little dog is like the Smooth Dachshund except for a beard and moustache that would look mighty distinguished curled and waxed. Most of our modern Dachshunds are so domesticated they couldn't tell a badger from a dusky-footed wood rat.

70
Dandie Dinmont Terrier
Weighs 14 to 24 pounds and is 8 to 11 inches high.

Sir Walter Scott wrote a novel called *Guy Mannering* in which he created a character called Dandie Dinmont. Dandie kept a couple of terriers of a type that later took on the name of Dandie Dinmont Terriers, all because of the popularity of the book. The dog orginated in the Scottish borders and nobody knows who the parents were.

71

Welsh Corgi (Cardigan and Pembroke)

The Cardigan weighs 15 to 25 pounds and is 12 inches high.
The Pembroke weighs 18 to 24 pounds and is 10 to 12 inches high.

In 1925, these dogs were shown as one breed in dog shows but in 1934, the English Kennel Club classified them separately. These lively little dogs were originally cattle drivers and would nip at the heels of the cattle to keep them in line.

Dogs with Flat Faces

72

Bulldog

Weighs 40 to 50 pounds and is about 15 inches high.

The sport of bull-baiting was started in England about 1209 and was finally abolished in 1835. The Bulldog developed a low-slung body to protect it from the thrusts of the bull. Its short nose and massive jaw helped it hang on for dear life while still being able to breathe. Breeders of today's Bulldog have eliminated all the ferocity and it is now as gentle as a powder puff.

73

Pekingese

Weighs under 14 pounds and is 6 to 10 inches high.

A sacred dog of China in ancient times, the theft of one was punishable by death. These little critters rode in style as they were carried about in the voluminous sleeves of the inhabitants of the royal palace. In 1860 four of them were smuggled out of China and one was given to Queen Victoria. It became the rage of the English court.

74

Boston Terrier

Weighs 12 to 25 pounds and is 16 inches high.

A proper Bostonian, the Boston Terrier is called the "American gentleman" among dogs. All it needs is a black tie and a top hat to complete the picture.

75

French Bulldog

Weighs 18 to 28 pounds and is about 12 inches high.

Some Toy Bulldogs were sent from England to France. Since the Bulldog is and always was British, they nearly came unglued when the French actually used the name and called it the French Bulldog.

76

Japanese Spaniel

Weighs about 7 pounds and is 9 inches high.

This dog was the pet of royalty and hobnobbed only with those of noble birth. Some of this must have rubbed off on this Spaniel as it looks royal enough to be sitting on a throne. One theory is that it originated in China and was sent as a present to the Emperor of Japan.

The Tallest Dogs

77

Great Dane

Weighs 120 to 150 pounds and is 28 to 34 inches high.

This dog has more dignity than an ambassador loaded with medals paying court to the British throne. It was in Germany that the breed reached its present standard of excellence; not in Denmark as the name implies. Originally, it was developed for the awesome task of destroying wild boar.

78

Scottish Deerhound

Weighs 75 to 110 pounds and is 28 to 32 inches high.

In days of yore, if you were of lesser rank than an Earl your chances of owning a Deerhound were absolutely ziltch. Sir Walter Scott, writer of romantic adventure, and Edward Landseer, animal painter, were great Deerhound fans and immortalized them in their works. Don't keep this royal dog penned up in an apartment where all it has to hunt is mice. Give it the wide-open spaces and the wild deer.

79
Borzoi (Russian Wolfhound)

Weighs 60 to 105 pounds and is 26 to 31 inches high.

Centuries ago, Russian aristocrats, accompanied by these magnificent dogs, looked like a Saks Fifth Avenue fashion show when they rode out to hunt. They were literally dressed to kill. Despite this bloodthirsty beginning the Borzoi breed is full of brotherly love for man and beast.

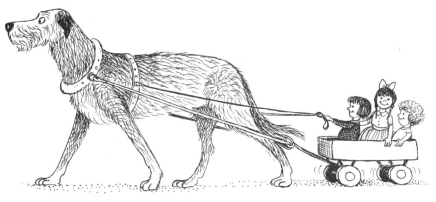

80
Irish Wolfhound

Weighs 105 to 140 pounds and is 30 to 40 inches high.

It is the tallest and probably the strongest of all dogs. As a result, it can afford to be very gentle and well-mannered. It is successful in wild boar and lion hunts but it is at its best when going after the big timber wolf and singly dispatching it.

Guard Dogs

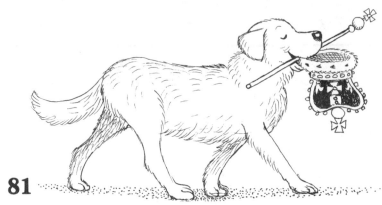

81
Kuvasz

Weighs about 70 pounds and is 24 to 27 inches high.

The great, great, great grandparents of this big, beautiful dog came from the high-flung domain of Tibet. But it was in Hungary that the Kuvasz developed into its present form. It guarded and saved many a royal master when so-called friends were clawing each others' hides for the other one's possessions.

82
Bull Mastiff

Weighs 100 to 115 pounds and is 24 to 27 inches high.

These dogs were developed when gamekeepers were having shootouts with the poachers. They wanted a dog that could handle a man like a Japanese wrestler and then hold him. They crossed a bulldog with a mastiff and—*Pow!*—there was the Bull Mastiff.

83
Mastiff

Weighs 165 to 185 pounds and is 27 to 33 inches high.

When the Romans invaded England in 55 B.C. many of them were given a tremendous mauling by these huge fighting dogs that fought right alongside their masters. When the Normans came in 1066, they found the Mastiff population quite numerous. This was before canned dog food and there were plenty of wolves around that served the Mastiff just as well.

84
Doberman Pinscher

Weighs 60 to 75 pounds and is 24 to 28 inches high.

A German by the name of Ludwig Dobermann founded the breed in 1890 by crossing a Shepherd and Rottweiler and adding a touch of Old English Terrier for good measure. Besides giving time to the war effort, the Doberman Pinscher became a crackerjack police dog.

85
German Shepherd
Weighs 60 to 85 pounds and is 23 to 25 inches high.

This dog is so willing to please that its ability to learn is tops. One of the first dog movie stars was Rin Tin Tin, a German Shepherd that made its master a lot of Yankee dollars by learning its acting part to perfection.

86
Giant Schnauzer
Weighs 75 pounds and is 21 to 25½ inches high.

If you viewed the Miniature Schnauzer through the zoom lens on your camera and enlarged its image, that's how the Giant Schnauzer would look (all three Schnauzer breeds look alike except for their sizes). It was originally developed in Bavaria for driving cattle and guarding stockyards.

The Pointers

87
English Setter

Weighs 50 to 70 pounds and is 23 to 25 inches high.

For over 400 years this beautiful dog has been pointing out birds. It can point out a bird faster than can a veteran Audubon bird watcher with high-powered binoculars.

88
Gordon Setter

Weighs 45 to 75 pounds and is 23 to 27 inches high.

The Gordon Setter is from Scotland and is named after the Duke of Gordon who spent a lifetime perfecting these beautiful dogs. On June 28, 1859, Gordon Setters participated in the world's first dog show. There was a real hassle over the fact that the judge's own dog, Dandy, was awarded the first prize.

89

Brittany Spaniel

Weighs 30 to 40 pounds and is 17½ to 20½ inches high.

This spaniel is the only pointing spaniel in the world. It locates its quarry by taking a good sniff of the wind and then—*Wam!*—it finds its bird and goes into its pointing act.

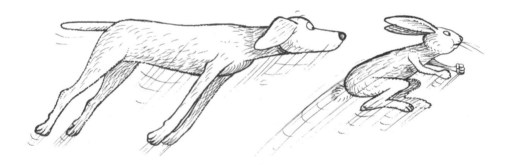

90

Vizsla

Weighs 40 to 60 pounds and is 21 to 24 inches high.

This large dog grew up on the plains of Hungary where bountiful crops of wheat, corn, and barley attracted hordes of game birds—plus the large Hungarian hare that made a mighty fine rabbit pie. The Vizsla was there to point them out.

91
Irish Setter

Weighs 50 to 60 pounds and is 23 to 26 inches high.

Everything this dog does it makes look very important. It is as fun-loving as a visitor at Disneyland and as good-looking as the winner of a beauty contest. As a result, it is bred for the dog show scene rather than being used as one of the most able of all the field dogs.

92
Weimaraner

Weighs 55 to 85 pounds and is 23 to 27 inches high.

If this dog knew what great qualifications it had to have in order to be a Weimaraner, it would pop all the buttons off its vest—that is, if it wore one. In short, the dog had to have good scenting ability, speed, courage, and intelligence.

93

Wire-haired Pointing Griffon

Weighs about 50 pounds and is 19½ to 23½ inches high.

In 1875, a certain F. K. Korthals, son of a wealthy Dutch banker and cattle breeder, bought a Griffon bitch and five other dogs. He no sooner started to breed them than his father objected to the raising of insignificant animals; namely, dogs. So Korthals took off in a cloud of dust for France where the major portion of the development of this dog took place. Its ability to point and retrieve game is tops.

94

Great Pyrenees

Weighs 90 to 125 pounds and is 25 to 32 inches high.

This huge dog not only looks after the sheep but his master as well. It is a great guide-dog on ski trips and was used to smuggle contraband over the Franco-Spanish border. It avoided customs officials by taking dangerous trails impossible for man to travel.

95

Newfoundland

Weighs 110 to 150 pounds and is 26 to 28 inches high.

Besides dragging carts, carrying packs, and hauling in nets, this gentle dog has rescued more men, women, and children by swimming in icy waters than you can shake a stick at.

96
St. Bernard Long-haired

Weighs about 170 pounds and is 25 to 29 inches high.

This great rescue dog has such an acute sense of smell that it can sniff out a man who is buried 20 feet under the snow. It has been working in the Alps for centuries as a guide dog.

(Also: Mastiff, 83; Otter Hound, 4; Great Dane, 77; and Irish Wolfhound, 80)

The Dog Show

97

Schipperke

Weighs under 18 pounds and is 12 to 13 inches high.

The Schipperke originated in the Flemish province of Belgium and the name in Flemish means "little captain." The title suits the dog perfectly as it stands guard on the deck of a canal boat. In 1885, Queen Marie Henriette acquired a Schipperke and from then on its popularity spread like honey on a piece of toast.

98

Siberian Husky

Weighs 35 to 50 pounds and is 20 to 23 inches high.

These bushy-tailed dogs were developed as sled dogs by the Eskimos of the Kolyma River in Siberia. Without the help of these wonderful dogs, they would have as much chance of survival as a sardine in the mouth of a salmon.

99
Welsh Springer Spaniel
Weighs 40 pounds and is about 17 inches high.

This is an old Welsh breed and much used as a hunting dog. It takes to the water like a small boy to an ice cream cone and can run after game in the roughest terrain. It is very gentle with children and other animals.

100
Bull Terrier
Weighs 25 to 60 pounds and is 19 to 23 inches high.

You can have your choice of either the white or the colored variety. They are otherwise the same. This is the gladiator of the canine ring and at one time was lucky if it lived from fight to fight. I am glad that dog-fighting has been abolished.

101

Poodle

Standard *weighs 45 to 55 pounds and is over 15 inches high.*
Miniature *weighs 10 pounds and is 10 to 15 inches high.*
Toy *weighs 7 pounds and is under 10 inches high.*

This popular dog was originally a fine hunter and swimmer. Its coat was trimmed to lighten its weight in the water. This started the vogue of fancy patterns in trimming. It is so French-looking you can almost hear it barking the Marseillaise. As a matter of fact, the French made it their national dog. The three varieties are identical except for size. Their ability to learn made them fine circus dogs.

102

English Toy Spaniel (King Charles Spaniel)

Weighs 9 to 12 pounds and is about 10 inches high.

King Charles II paid more attention to his Toy Spaniel than he did to the affairs of state and as a result the dog took on his name. Gainsborough, Rubens, and Rembrandt have painted these little critters with their fashionable sitters.

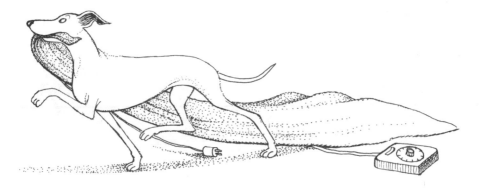

103
Italian Greyhound

Weighs 6 to 10 pounds and is about 10 inches high.

It looks exactly like the Greyhound except that it is half the size.
In fact, some of the rabbits the Greyhound chases at the races
are nearly as big as this little dog. They love the comforts of the
fireside, the sofa and its cushions and above all, the warm lap
of its owner.

104
Brussels Griffon

Weighs 5 to 12 pounds and is about 8 inches high.

To begin with, these dogs specialized in decreasing the rat
population in the stables. But, being ambitious, and having a
strong sense of self-importance, they soon found themselves in
the driver's seat of a hansom cab, next to their master. From
this superior position they appointed themselves guards.

105
Papillon
Weighs 5 to 11 pounds and is 11 inches high.

This little dog's ears look like a butterfly in flight, which gave it the French name Papillon. It was made popular by the Marquise de Pompadour, plus other ladies of the French court who often had their portraits painted holding their pet Papillon.

106
Short-haired St. Bernard
Weighs 170 pounds and is 25 to 29 inches high.

You could fill a good-sized auditorium with people this magnificent dog has saved in the last three centuries—2,500 people to be exact. This includes those saved by the Rough-coated St. Bernard. Despite the giant meals these animals consume, 27,000 of them are registered annually in the United States.

107

Alaskan Malamute

Weighs 50 to 85 pounds and is 20 to 25 inches high.

This old breed of Arctic sled dog was named after the Malamute tribe in Alaska. These people, who developed the breed, were "upper strata" and treated their dogs with the respect they deserved. Without these wonderful dogs, travel would be as limited as a fly's takeoff from a strip of sticky fly paper.

108

Harrier

Weighs 40 to 50 pounds and is 19 to 21 inches high.

Nobody can accuse the Harrier of being fickle in its occupation of hunting hares, because it has been doing just that since 400 B.C. What it doesn't know about hares you could stuff in the eye of a flea.

109

Rhodesian Ridgeback

Weighs 65 to 75 pounds and is 24 to 27 inches high.

This native South African is often called the African Lion Hound. Its characteristic feature is the ridge on its back caused by the hair growing in a direction opposite to that of the rest of the coat. In other words, this dog's hair stands on end even before the dog has seen a lion. Besides being a great hunter it is a devoted family dog.

110

Sussex Spaniel

Weighs 35 to 45 pounds and is 16 inches high.

A turtle would give this dog a run for its money as far as speed is concerned. But it makes up for this with his wonderful sniffing ability and great determination. It can be trained to be an excellent retriever.

111
Bernese Mountain Dog
Weighs 50 to 75 pounds and is 21 to 27½ inches high.

Two thousand years ago, in Switzerland, these aristocratic-looking dogs were left by the invading Roman soldiers. Soon after this, the dogs took a few jobs away from the donkey by hauling small carts.

112
American Staffordshire Terrier
Weighs 30 to 50 pounds and is 17 to 19 inches.

In the United States the name of this breed was changed on January 1, 1972, from Stafford Terrier to American Staffordshire Terrier. This dog has had its name changed more times than a man most-wanted by the F.B.I. It has been called Bull-and-terrier dog, Half-and-Half, Pit Dog or Pit Bullterrier, American Bull Terrier, and Yankee Terrier. Long ago they were in the fight game which is now, thankfully, outlawed.

Numerical Listing:

Gurney's Gallery of Dogs
(The Order in Which They Appear in the Text)

The Shaggiest Dogs
1. Affenpinscher
2. Old English Sheepdog
3. Briard
4. Otter Hound
5. Puli

Dogs with Tails that Curl Over Their Backs
6. Shih Tzu
7. Lhasa Apso
8. Norwegian Elkhound
9. Samoyed
10. Keeshond
11. Chow Chow
12. Basenji
13. Pug

Sheep Dogs
14. Border Collie
15. Komondor
16. Bearded Collie
17. Collie
18. Shetland Sheepdog
19. Belgian Sheepdog
20. Belgian Malinois
21. Belgian Tervuren
22. Rottweiler

The Smallest Dogs

23. Chihuahua
24. Maltese
25. Pomeranian
26. Yorkshire Terrier

Dogs with Curly Coats

27. American Water Spaniel
28. Curly-coated Retriever
29. Bedlington Terrier

Dogs with Spots

30. Dalmatian
31. German Short-haired Pointer
32. Pointer

Dogs with the Most Handsome Beards

33. Airedale Terrier
34. Sealyham Terrier
35. Lakeland Terrier
36. West Highland White Terrier
37. Standard Schnauzer
38. Wire-haired Fox Terrier
39. Kerry Blue Terrier
40. Welsh Terrier
41. Bouvier des Flandres
42. Scottish Terrier

More Terriers

Retrievers

The Fastest Dogs

The Greatest Sniffers

Dogs with the Shortest Legs

67. Long-haired Dachshund
68. Smooth Dachshund
69. Wire-haired Dachshund
70. Dandie Dinmont Terrier
71. Welsh Corgi (Cardigan, Pembroke)

Dogs with Flat Faces

72. Bulldog
73. Pekingese
74. Boston Terrier
75. French Bulldog
76. Japanese Spaniel
   (Also: Pug, 13)

The Tallest Dogs

77. Great Dane
78. Scottish Deerhound
79. Borzoi (Russian Wolfhound)
80. Irish Wolfhound

Guard Dogs

81. Kuvasz
82. Bull Mastiff
83. Mastiff
84. Doberman Pinscher
85. German Shepherd
86. Giant Schnauzer

The Pointers
87. English Setter
88. Gordon Setter
89. Brittany Spaniel
90. Vizsla
91. Irish Setter
92. Weimaraner
93. Wire-haired Pointing Griffon
   (Also: The Pointer, 32)

The Heaviest Dogs
94. Great Pyrenees
95. Newfoundland
96. St. Bernard Long-haired
   (Also: Mastiff, 83; Otter Hound, 4;
      Great Dane 77; Irish Wolfhound, 80)

The Dog Show
97. Schipperke
98. Siberian Husky
99. Welsh Springer Spaniel
100. Bull Terrier
101. Poodle
102. English Toy Spaniel
103. Italian Greyhound
104. Brussels Griffon
105. Papillon
106. Short-haired St. Bernard
107. Alaskan Malamute
108. Harrier
109. Rhodesian Ridgeback
110. Sussex Spaniel
111. Bernese Mountain Dog
112. American Staffordshire Terrier

Alphabetical Listing

Gurney's Gallery of Dogs

(Numbered According to the Text)

Affenpinscher (1)
Afghan Hound (60)
Airedale Terrier (33)
Alaskan Malamute (107)
American Staffordshire Terrier (112)
American Water Spaniel (27)
Australian Terrier (46)
Basenji (12)
Basset Hound (63)
Beagle (65)
Bearded Collie (16)
Bedlington Terrier (29)
Belgian Malinois (20)
Belgian Sheepdog (19)
Belgian Tervuren (21)
Bernese Mountain Dog (111)
Black and Tan Coonhound (64)
Bloodhound (66)
Border Collie (14)
Border Terrier (43)
Borzoi (79)

Boston Terrier (74)
Bouvier des Flandres (41)
Briard (3)
Brittany Spaniel (89)
Brussels Griffon (104)
Bull Mastiff (82)
Bull Terrier (100)
Bulldog (72)
Cairn Terrier (44)
Chesapeake Bay Retriever (51)
Chihuahua (23)
Chow Chow (11
Cocker Spaniel (57)
Collie (17)
Curly-coated Retriever (28)
Dachshund, Long-haired (67)
Dachshund, Smooth (68)
Dachshund, Wire-haired (69)
Dalmatian (30)
Dandie Dinmont Terrier (70)
Doberman Pinscher (84)
English Setter (87)
English Springer Spaniel (54)
English Toy Spaniel (102)
Flat-coated Retriever (55)
Foxhound (62)
French Bulldog (75

German Shepherd (85)
German Short-haired Pointer (31)
Giant Schnauzer (86)
Golden Retriever (53)
Gordon Setter (88)
Great Dane (77)
Great Pyrenees (94)
Greyhound (59)
Harrier (108)
Irish Setter (91)
Irish Terrier (47)
Irish Water Spaniel (52)
Irish Wolfhound (80)
Italian Greyhound (103)
Japanese Spaniel (76)
Keeshond (10)
Kerry Blue Terrier (39)
Komondor (15)
Kuvasz (81)
Labrador Retriever (56)
Lakeland Terrier (35)
Lhasa Apso (7)
Maltese (24)
Manchester Terrier (49)
Mastiff (83)

Newfoundland (95)
Norwegian Elkhound (8)
Norwich Terrier (48)
Old English Sheepdog (2)
Otter Hound (4)
Papillon (105)
Pekingese (73)
Pointer (32)
Pomeranian (25)
Poodle (101)
Pug (13)
Puli (5)
Rhodesian Ridgeback (109)
Rottweiler (22)
Russian Wolfhound (Borzoi) (79)
St. Bernard Long-haired (96)
Short-haired St. Bernard (106)
Saluki (61)
Samoyed (9)
Schipperke (97)
Schnauzer, Standard (37)
Schnauzer, Giant (86)
Scottish Deerhound (78)
Scottish Terrier (42)
Sealyham Terrier (42)
Shetland Sheepdog (18)

Shih Tzu (6)
Siberian Husky (98)
Silky Terrier (45)
Smooth Fox Terrier (50)
Sussex Spaniel (110)
Vizsla (90)
Weimaraner (92)
Welsh Corgi (Cardigan, Pembroke) (71)
Welsh Springer Spaniel (99)
Welsh Terrier (40)
West Highland White Terrier (36)
Whippet (58)
Wire-haired Fox Terrier (38)
Wire-haired Pointing Griffon (93)
Yorkshire Terrier (26)

. . . and the Most Popular Dog of Them All—

THE MUTT